ROSWELL

by Ellis M. Reed

CAPSTONE PRESS
a capstone imprint

Bright Idea Books are published by Capstone Press
1710 Roe Crest Drive, North Mankato, Minnesota 56003
www.mycapstone.com

Library of Congress Cataloging-in-Publication Data
Names: Reed, Ellis M., 1992- author.
Title: Roswell / by Ellis M. Reed.
Description: North Mankato, Minnesota: Bright Idea Books are published by
    Capstone Press, [2020] | Series: Aliens | Includes index. | Audience: Grade 4 to 6.
Identifiers: LCCN 2018060988 (print) | LCCN 2019000662 (ebook) | ISBN
    9781543571158 (ebook) | ISBN 9781543571073 (hardcover) | ISBN 9781543574944 (pbk.)
Subjects: LCSH: Roswell Incident, Roswell, N.M., 1947--Juvenile literature. |
    Unidentified flying objects--Sightings and encounters--New Mexico--Roswell
    Region--Juvenile literature. | Military research--United States--Juvenile literature.
Classification: LCC TL789.5.N6 (ebook) | LCC TL789.5.N6 R44 2020 (print) |
    DDC 001.94209789/43--dc23
LC record available at https://lccn.loc.gov/2018060988

All internet sites appearing in back matter were available and accurate when this book was sent to press.

Editorial Credits
Editor: Claire Vanden Branden
Designer: Becky Daum
Production Specialist: Melissa Martin

Photo Credits
Alamy: Brian Cahn/Zuma Press, Inc., 27, Chronicle, 6–7, Stocktrek Images, Inc., 19; iStockphoto: ktsimage, 12–13, Mlenny, 15, SWInsider, 25; Newscom: World History Archive, 9; Shutterstock Images: adike, 31, Everett Historical, 20–21, Fer Gregory, cover (spaceship), Gianni Caponera, 22–23, 29, Mette Fairgrieve, 11, 28, photoBeard, 16–17, RebeccaPavlik, 5, Thomas Pajot, cover (sign)

Design Elements: Shutterstock Images, Red Line Editorial

Printed in the United States of America.
PA70

TABLE OF CONTENTS

CHAPTER 1

A STRANGE Object

Mac Brazel owned a ranch outside Roswell, New Mexico. He had many animals. One day in 1947 Brazel went out to feed his sheep. But he saw something very strange. A large object had crashed on his land.

Mac Brazel lived on a ranch nearly 80 miles (129 kilometers) from Roswell, New Mexico.

Two men examine a strange object that has fallen from the sky.

THE OBJECT

Brazel got closer to the object. It was made of metal sticks. The object was pieced together with tape. There were scraps that looked like paper. There were also big pieces of strange fabrics. Brazel saw foil too.

Brazel did not know what it was.

He called the sheriff in Roswell.

The sheriff looked at it. But he did not

know what it was either. So he called the

Roswell Army Air Field (RAAF).

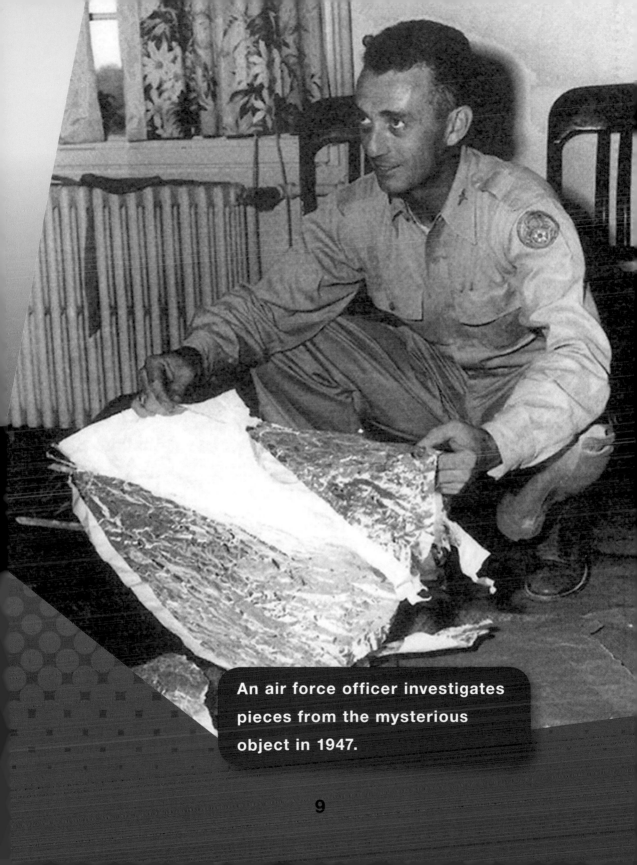

An air force officer investigates pieces from the mysterious object in 1947.

CHAPTER 2

WEATHER
Balloon

RAAF soldiers came to Brazel's farm. They looked at the object. Then they took it back to their base.

The *Roswell Daily Record* ran a story about the object. The story called the object a flying saucer. But the RAAF made a statement the next day. It said the object wasn't a flying saucer. It was a **weather balloon.**

Weather balloons are put into the air to gather information on air temperatures and wind speeds.

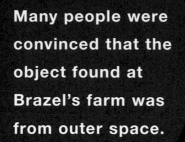

Many people were convinced that the object found at Brazel's farm was from outer space.

But people were not sure. They said it did not look like a weather balloon. Many thought the government was hiding something. They thought the object was an **alien** spaceship.

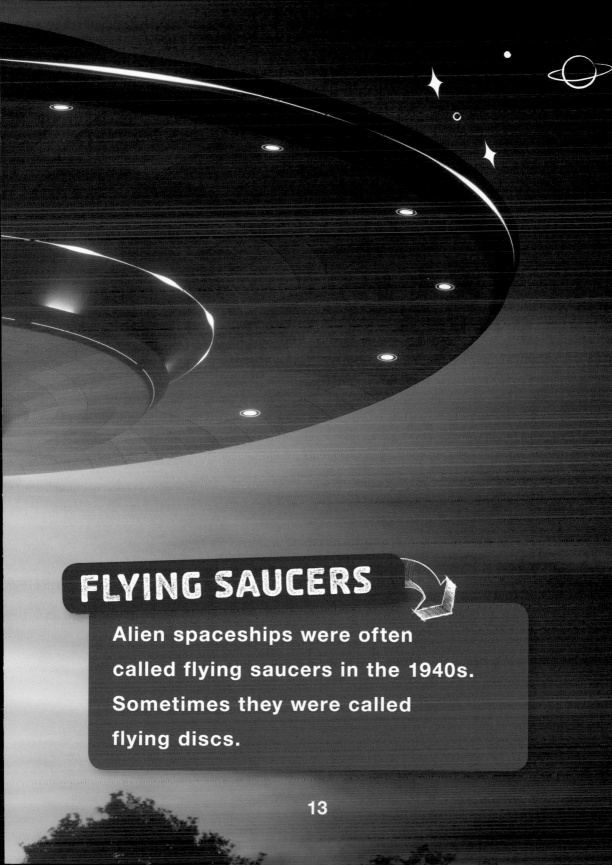

FLYING SAUCERS

Alien spaceships were often called flying saucers in the 1940s. Sometimes they were called flying discs.

CHAPTER 3

MORE Lies

Years later the government ran tests near Roswell. These tests used dummies. The dummies looked like people. Many thought they were really alien bodies. They believed the government was hiding things again.

The government used dummies to test how high pilots could fall from the sky and still survive.

THE VIDEO

Ray Santilli made a video in 1995. There were three government workers. They were in strange suits. They were cutting up a dead body. The body was an alien. It was said to be from the 1947 crash. The video was in black and white. It was 17 minutes long.

People thought the video was real. Ten years later Santilli said he had lied. The video was fake. He said it was based off a real video. He had just remade it. But the whole thing was a lie.

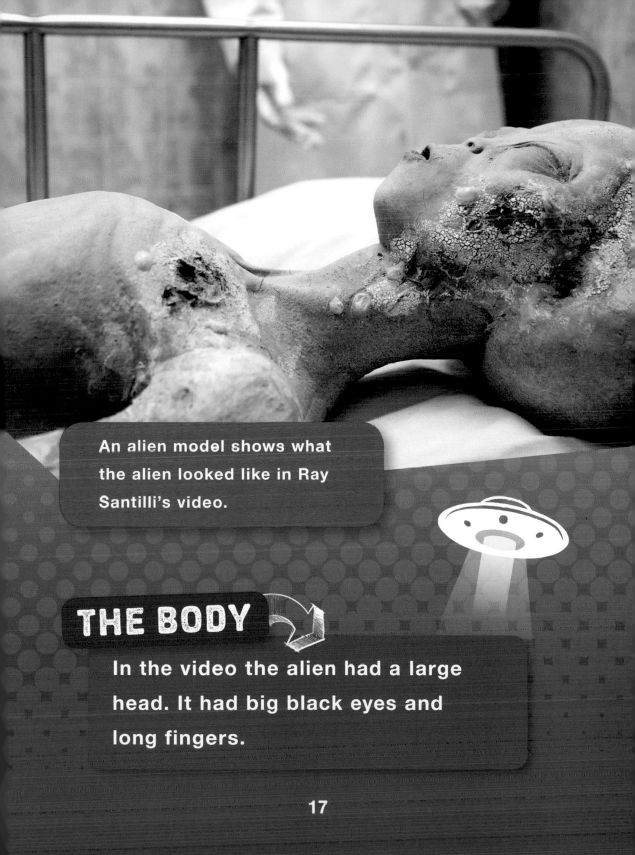

An alien model shows what the alien looked like in Ray Santilli's video.

THE BODY

In the video the alien had a large head. It had big black eyes and long fingers.

CHAPTER 4

THE
Truth

Many years passed. The air force finally told the truth. It said the object was not a weather balloon. So what was it?

The air force told people about Project Mogul. It was a secret army project. Only the government knew about it.

The U.S. Air Force has many bases in New Mexico. The government uses these as airfields for military planes.

The government made special balloons. They had microphones. These listened for sound waves from bombs. The government was worried about the Soviet Union. It thought the Soviets might attack the United States. It wanted to know if an attack was coming.

The balloons were meant to sense atomic bombs. The U.S. and the Soviet Union both built these bombs in the 1940s and 1950s.

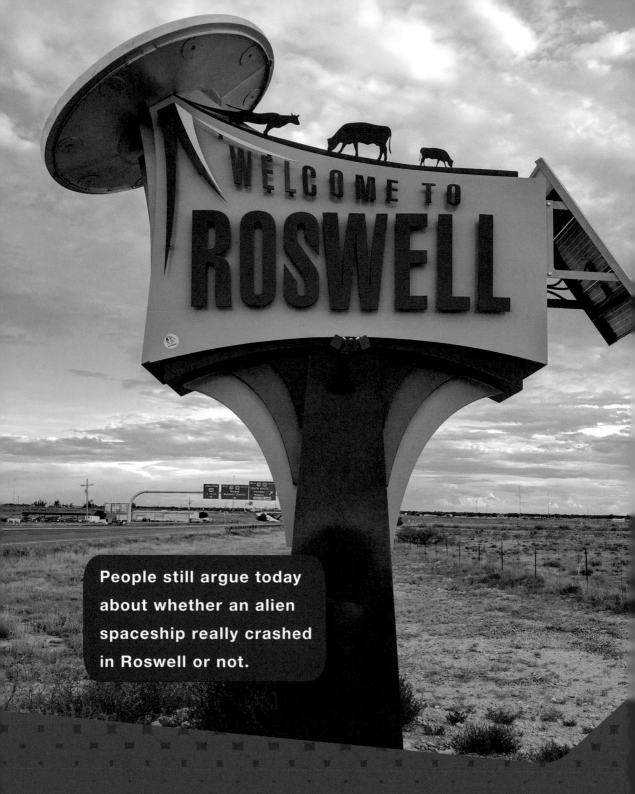

People still argue today about whether an alien spaceship really crashed in Roswell or not.

The object in Roswell was part of this secret project. The government could not tell people before. So it said the object was a weather balloon. But many people still think it lied.

CHAPTER 5

ROSWELL
Today

People still look for aliens in Roswell. The International **UFO** Museum and Research Center is there. It opened in 1992. It tells people about UFO history.

The International UFO Museum and Research Center has many different UFO exhibits.

Roswell also has the UFO Festival every year. In 2018 more than 20,000 people came. People watch movies. They listen to people give speeches. They talk to each other about aliens. They even make arts and crafts.

The government said there are no aliens in Roswell. But people still remember the event from 1947. Some still want to prove the government found aliens.

One part of the annual UFO festival includes a costume contest.

GLOSSARY

alien
a creature not from Earth

UFO
unidentified flying object

weather balloon
a balloon that is sent into
the air to gather information
about the weather

TRIVIA

1. The first use of the term "flying saucer" was in June 1947. Pilot Kenneth Arnold saw strange lights in the sky. He told the local newspaper that they flew like a saucer. The newspaper reported that Arnold had seen "flying saucers."

2. Files from the Roswell Air Force base went missing in 1947. No one knows who took the files or what they were trying to hide.

ACTIVITY

HAVE A DEBATE

Many people have heard about the UFO in Roswell. They may have formed strong opinions about what really happened. Some people don't believe that it was really Project Mogul. They think that the object was an alien spaceship. People argue their opinions. They try to convince others. This is known as a debate.

Pick a side in the Roswell debate. Find three pieces of evidence that support your argument. Then think about a friend who would be on the other side. What three pieces of evidence might they come up with? How would you respond to their evidence?

FURTHER RESOURCES

Interested in learning more about space?
Check out these resources:

NASA Space Place: Build Your Own Spacecraft!
https://spaceplace.nasa.gov/build-a-spacecraft/en

Peake, Tim. *Hello, Is This Planet Earth? My View from the International Space Station*. New York: Little, Brown and Company, 2017.

Want to know about other alien beliefs?
Take a look at these resources:

ESA Kids: Life Beyond Earth
https://www.esa.int/kids/en/learn/Life_in_Space/Are_we_alone/Life_beyond_ Earth

Reed, Ellis M. *Alien Conspiracy Theories*. Aliens. North Mankato, Minn.: Capstone Press, 2020.

INDEX